THE cupcake BOOK

THE *cupcake* BOOK

Susanna Tee

Ivy Press

This edition first published in the UK in 2008 by

Ivy Press

The Old Candlemakers

West Street, Lewes

East Sussex, BN7 2NZ, UK

www.ivy-group.co.uk

ISBN 13: 978-1-905695-63-8

ISBN 10: 1-905695-63-2

Printed and bound in Thailand

This book was conceived, designed, and produced by

iBall, an imprint of

Ivy Press

Creative Director **Peter Bridgewater**

Publisher **Jason Hook**

Editorial Director **Caroline Earle**

Art Director **Sarah Howerd**

Senior Project Editor **Dominique Page**

Project Designer **Joanna Clinch**

Photographer **Andrew Perris**

Illustrator **Melvyn Evans**

Food Economist **Colin Capon**

acknowledgements

Ivy Press would like to thank the following

for kindly lending props:

Steamer Trading, Lewes, East Sussex, UK

Bright Ideas, Lewes, East Sussex, UK

contents

introduction

Cupcakes, also known as fairy cakes, are the little darlings of the cake world – exquisite, tiny, delicious mouthfuls that are just enough to satisfy your cake-lust, but not enough to weigh you down. Decorated to suit the occasion, they are the perfect treat for any age or occasion, whether it is Mother's Day, a child's birthday party, a wedding, a dinner party, a cake sale or your mid-morning coffee break.

So how did cupcakes come into the world? Some say it is because the ingredients used to make them were all measured by the cup; others say that they were baked in tea cups, or little fluted moulds in fancy shapes, in order to cook them more quickly than large cakes. Whatever the explanation, they have been with us since the eighteenth century. The first commercial cupcake was produced by the Hostess Company in 1919.

In this book you have many choices. There are classic cupcakes, such as sticky gingerbread, children's favourite peanut butter, and moist carrot cake; there are fruit and nut cupcakes, such as indulgent fresh strawberry, tasty apple sauce, and sweet lemon cheesecake; and there are the decadent chocolate cupcakes, such as gooey chocolate brownies, rich chocolate cherry and creamy white chocolate chip.

Look for different decorations. There is a wide variety available, from sprinkles and small silver or gold balls to sugared or elaborate chocolate flowers. Or create your own stencils and simply sprinkle with icing sugar. But why waste time reading about them when you could be eating them? These dainty desserts are easy to make – with just a few basic ingredients and a little creativity, you can whip up a batch in no time at all.

what you'll need

You don't needs lots of fancy equipment to make cupcakes. To make the 25 seriously scrumptious recipes in this book, you'll need fluted paper baking cups, a variety of decorating stencils to dust sugar designs, a star-shaped nozzle and an icing bag.

Baking cups

Fluted paper or foil baking cups retain the cupcakes. They are available in various colours as well as sizes; the standard ones vary in size and mini and muffin cups are also available. For a generous cupcake, we've used American-style baking cups in the recipes (available from specialized cook shops) which are twice the size of English cupcake cases. This also gives you more room to be creative with stencils and decoration (see pages 62–64)! If you do prefer the more genteel English cupcake, note that the cases will make double the quantity and you should reduce baking times by 5–10 minutes. You can also buy flexible ovenware moulds in standard and mini sizes made from heat-resistant non-stick silicone. To test if the cupcakes are cooked, insert a cocktail stick in the centre; it should come out clean when they are done.

Icing nozzles

A star nozzle is for creating swirls or rosettes of butter cream or whipped double cream on top of the cupcakes. A small round writing nozzle can be used for spreading melted chocolate or icing made with icing sugar, thinned with a little water to a coating consistency. Place your chosen nozzle in the icing bag, fill the bag no more than half full and twist or fold to seal the filling. Hold the bag at a 45-degree angle and squeeze gently to release icing from the nozzle.

Decorating stencils

Decorating stencils add a lovely finishing touch to your cupcake creation. You can buy these in a variety of designs or why not make your own? (See pages 62–63 for instructions and ideas.) Hold the stencil closely over the top of the cupcake, positioning it where you wish the design to fall. If necessary, place a small square of white paper below the pattern you are not using, to prevent the sugar from falling through. Dredge with either icing sugar or cocoa powder, then when the dust has settled, carefully lift off the stencil to reveal the pattern. Stencil your cupcakes shortly before serving, so that the pattern does not fade as it is absorbed by the moist cupcake.

FLOWERS   HEARTS   STARS

cupcake fest

classic cupcakes

Chocolate Chip

Peanut Butter

Black Bottom

Carrot Cake

Classic Vanilla

Buttermilk Spice

Honey and Orange

Gingerbread

fruit & nut cupcakes

Fresh Strawberry

Blueberry

Lemon Ginger

Mixed Fruit

Lemon Cheesecake

Apple Sauce

Pecan

Banana and Walnut

Peach

Almond and Orange

chocolate cupcakes

Chocolate Brownies

Chocolate Courgette

Cherry Chocolate

Mocha Cappuccino

White Chocolate Chip

Cream-filled Chocolate

Chocolate Fudge

chocolate chip

Easy to make, these are a popular choice with all ages. As a variation, replace the plain chocolate chips with white chocolate or raisins.

you will need

450 g (1 lb) plain white flour
5 tsp baking powder
175 g (6 oz) butter, softened
200 g (7 oz) caster sugar
4 eggs
4 tbsp milk
200 g (7 oz) plain chocolate chips

❀ Preheat the oven to 180°C/350°F/Gas Mark 4. Line muffin pans with 18 fluted paper baking cups. Sift together the flour and baking powder.

❀ Put the butter and sugar in a large bowl and whisk until light and fluffy. Add the eggs, one at a time, beating well after each addition. Fold the sifted flour mixture into the batter, then the milk and the chocolate chips.

❀ Fill each baking cup with the batter. Bake in the oven for about 25 minutes until golden brown and firm to the touch. Leave the cupcakes in the pans for 10 minutes, then transfer to a wire rack to cool completely.

peanut butter

Packed with peanut butter and topped with a peanut butter icing, there's more than enough to satisfy the most ardent peanut butter fan – a true favourite, especially with children.

you will need

225 g (8 oz) plain white flour
2 tsp baking powder
55 g (2 oz) butter, softened
225 g (8 oz) soft light brown sugar
115 g (4 oz) crunchy peanut butter
2 eggs
¾ tsp vanilla extract
100 ml (3½ fl oz) milk

for the topping

150 g (5½ oz) crunchy peanut butter
55 g (2 oz) full-fat soft cream cheese
25 g (1 oz) butter, softened
225 g (8 oz) icing sugar

✿ Preheat the oven to 180°C/350°F/Gas Mark 4. Line muffin pans with 14 fluted paper baking cups. Sift together the flour and baking powder.

✿ Put the butter, brown sugar and peanut butter in a large bowl and whisk for 1–2 minutes until well mixed. Add the eggs, one at a time, beating well after each addition, then beat in the vanilla extract. Using a large metal spoon, fold in the flour mixture and then the milk.

✿ Fill each baking cup with the batter and bake in the oven for about 25 minutes until golden brown and firm to the touch. Leave the cupcakes in the pans for 10 minutes, then transfer to a wire rack to cool completely.

✿ For the topping, beat together the peanut butter, cream cheese and butter until smooth. Sift in the icing sugar and beat until well mixed.

✿ When the cupcakes are cool, spread the icing on top of each, swirling it gently with a small round-bladed knife.

black bottom

These classic cupcakes, with a very tasty centre of cream cheese and chocolate chips, are rich and deliciously gooey – a real treat for those with a sweet tooth.

you will need

225 g (8 oz) plain white flour

1 tsp bicarbonate of soda

3½ tbsp cocoa powder

275 g (9½ oz) caster sugar

250 ml (9 fl oz) water

5 tbsp sunflower oil

1 tbsp white vinegar

1 tsp vanilla extract

200 g (7 oz) full-fat soft cream cheese

1 egg

150 g (5½ oz) plain chocolate chips

✿ Preheat the oven to 180°C/350°F/Gas Mark 4. Line muffin pans with 16 fluted paper baking cups and generously spray the inside of the cups with a non-stick cooking spray. Sift together the flour, bicarbonate of soda and cocoa powder.

✿ Stir in 200 g (7 oz) of the sugar into the flour mixture and make a well in the centre. Mix together the water, oil, vinegar and vanilla and pour into the well. Mix thoroughly and pour the batter into a jug.

✿ Put the cream cheese, egg and remaining sugar in a bowl and beat together until light and fluffy. Stir in the chocolate chips.

✿ Pour the mixture from the jug to fill each baking cup no more than two-thirds full. Top with a dollop of the cream cheese mixture and bake in the oven for about 25 minutes until firm to the touch. Leave in the pans for 10 minutes, then transfer to a wire rack to cool completely.

carrot cake

12 APPROX

It is the subtle addition of healthy grated carrots and orange juice that makes these cupcakes so incredibly moist. A hint of spice is the perfect complement.

you will need

225 g (8 oz) plain white flour

1 tsp baking powder

½ tsp bicarbonate of soda

2 tsp ground mixed spice

150 ml (¼ pint) sunflower oil

4 eggs

175 g (6 oz) soft light brown sugar

175 g (6 oz) grated carrots

50 g (2 oz) walnut pieces, roughly chopped

2 tbsp orange juice

for the topping

280 g (10 oz) soft cream cheese

4 tbsp icing sugar

shredded zest of 2 oranges

❀ Preheat the oven to 180°C/350°F/Gas Mark 4. Line a muffin pan with 12 fluted paper baking cups and spray cups generously with a non-stick cooking spray. Sift together the flour, baking powder, bicarbonate of soda and mixed spice.

❀ Put the oil, eggs and brown sugar in a large bowl and whisk, then add the flour mixture. Squeeze any liquid from the carrots, then fold them into the mixture with the walnuts and juice.

❀ Fill each baking cup with the batter and bake in the oven for about 25 minutes until well risen and firm to the touch. Leave in the pan for 10 minutes, then transfer to a wire rack to cool completely.

❀ For the topping, put the cream cheese and icing sugar in a large bowl and beat together until light and fluffy.

❀ When the cupcakes are cool, spread the icing over each. Chill in the fridge until ready to serve, then decorate with shredded orange zest.

classic vanilla

This is a classic cupcake recipe that you will turn to time and time again. Decorate them as simply or as lavishly as you like to suit the occasion.

you will need

375 g (13 oz) plain white flour

1 tsp baking powder

115 g (4 oz) butter, softened

200 g (7 oz) caster sugar

3 eggs

1½ tsp vanilla extract

175 ml (6 fl oz) milk

for the topping

175 g (6 oz) butter, softened

350 g (12 oz) icing sugar

2 tbsp milk

6 drops vanilla extract

coloured sprinkles or edible sugar shapes for decorating

❀ Preheat the oven to 180°C/350°F/Gas Mark 4. Line muffin pans with 16 fluted paper baking cups. Sift together the flour and baking powder.

❀ Put the butter and caster sugar in a large bowl and whisk until light and fluffy. Add the eggs, one at a time, beating well after each addition, then beat in the vanilla. Using a large metal spoon, fold in the flour mixture and then the milk.

❀ Fill each baking cup with the batter and bake in the oven for about 25 minutes until golden brown and firm to the touch. Leave the cupcakes in the pans for 10 minutes, then transfer to a wire rack to cool completely.

❀ For the topping, beat the butter until light and fluffy. Sift in the icing sugar and beat until smooth, adding the milk and vanilla extract.

❀ When the cupcakes are cool, pipe the icing on top of each using an icing bag fitted with a star nozzle, then decorate as you wish.

buttermilk spice

Buttermilk conjures up old-fashioned home cooking, and these lightly spiced buttermilk cupcakes are certainly a time-tested favourite.

you will need

300 g (10½ oz) plain white flour

1 tsp baking powder

½ tsp bicarbonate of soda

1 tsp ground cinnamon

1 tsp ground ginger

½ tsp ground mixed spice

½ tsp grated nutmeg

180 g (6½ oz) butter, softened

200 g (7 oz) soft dark brown sugar

2 large eggs

200 ml (7 fl oz) buttermilk

sifted icing sugar, for dusting

❀ Preheat the oven to 180°C/350°F/Gas Mark 4. Line muffin pans with 18 fluted paper baking cups and spray cups generously with non-stick cooking spray. Sift together the flour, baking powder, bicarbonate of soda, cinnamon, ginger, mixed spice and nutmeg.

❀ Put the butter and brown sugar in a large bowl and whisk until light and fluffy. Add the eggs, one at a time, beating well after each addition. Using a large metal spoon, fold in the flour mixture, then fold in the buttermilk.

❀ Fill each baking cup with the batter and bake in the oven for about 30 minutes until golden brown and firm to the touch. Leave the cupcakes in the pans for 10 minutes, then transfer to a wire rack to cool completely.

❀ Dust with sifted icing sugar just before serving to decorate.

honey and orange

Flavoured with honey, orange and spices and topped with delicious cream and honey swirls, these cupcakes are dense, moist and oh-so decadent.

you will need

225 g (8 oz) plain white flour

1 tsp baking powder

½ tsp ground cinnamon

large pinch ground cloves

large pinch grated nutmeg

175 g (6 oz) butter, softened

200 g (7 oz) caster sugar

4 tbsp flavoured clear honey, such as orange blossom

grated rind of 2 oranges

4 eggs

for the topping

200 ml (7 fl oz) double cream

3 tsp flavoured clear honey, such as orange blossom

2 oranges, thinly sliced

✿ Preheat the oven to 190°C/375°F/Gas Mark 5. Line muffin pans with 14 fluted paper baking cups and spray cups generously with a non-stick cooking spray. Sift together the flour, baking powder, cinnamon, cloves and nutmeg.

✿ Put the butter and caster sugar in a large bowl and whisk until light and fluffy. Beat in the honey and rind. Add the eggs, one at a time, beating well after each addition. Using a large metal spoon, fold in the flour mixture.

✿ Fill each baking cup with the batter and bake in the oven for about 25 minutes until golden brown and firm to the touch. Leave the cupcakes in the pans for 10 minutes, then transfer to a wire rack to cool completely.

✿ For the topping, whisk the cream until it holds its shape, then fold in the honey.

✿ When the cupcakes are cool, use a piping bag fitted with a star nozzle to pipe swirls of the honey cream on top of each cupcake, then decorate with a twisted orange slice.

gingerbread

Sticky, just as gingerbread should be, these melt-in-the-mouth cupcakes are topped with a delicious ginger buttercream for true indulgence.

you will need

225 g (8 oz) plain white flour

4 tsp ground ginger

1½ tsp ground cinnamon

2 pieces preserved ginger in syrup

1½ tsp bicarbonate of soda

125 ml (4 fl oz) milk

175 g (6 oz) butter, softened

140 g (5 oz) soft dark brown sugar

4 tbsp black treacle

4 eggs

for the topping

6 oz (175 g) butter, softened

350 g (12 oz) icing sugar

4 tbsp ginger syrup from the jar

4 pieces stem ginger in syrup

✿ Preheat the oven to 170°C/325°F/Gas Mark 3. Line muffin pans with 20 fluted paper baking cups and spray cups generously with a non-stick cooking spray. Sift together the flour, ground ginger and cinnamon. Finely chop the stem ginger, then stir in the flour mix until well coated. Dissolve the bicarbonate of soda in the milk.

✿ Put the butter and brown sugar in a large bowl and whisk until light and fluffy. Beat in the treacle, then add the eggs, one at a time, beating well after each addition. Beat in the flour mixture, then gradually beat in the milk.

✿ Fill each baking cup with the batter and bake in the oven for about 25 minutes until golden brown and firm to the touch. Leave the cupcakes in the pans for 10 minutes, then transfer to a wire rack to cool completely.

✿ For the topping, beat the butter until light and fluffy. Sift in the icing sugar, add the syrup then beat until smooth.

✿ When the cupcakes are cool, use a star nozzle to pipe the icing on top of each, then sprinkle with finely chopped ginger.

fresh strawberry

18 APPROX

Cupcakes made with fresh strawberries are always a favourite, but they are equally good made with other red berry fruits, any tartness offset by a rich cream topping.

you will need

400 g (14 oz) plain white flour

1 tsp bicarbonate of soda

225 ml (8 fl oz) sunflower oil

2 eggs

200 g (7 oz) caster sugar

½ tsp vanilla extract

300 g (10½ oz) fresh strawberries, crushed

for the topping

300 ml (½ pint) double cream

18 small whole fresh strawberries

sifted icing sugar, for dusting

✿ Preheat the oven to 180°C/350°F/Gas Mark 4. Line muffin pans with 18 fluted paper baking cups. Sift together the flour and bicarbonate of soda.

✿ Put the oil, eggs, caster sugar and vanilla in a large bowl and whisk. Mix in the flour mixture then, using a large metal spoon, fold in the strawberries.

✿ Fill each baking cup with the batter and bake in the oven for about 30 minutes until golden brown and firm to the touch. Leave the cupcakes in the pans for 10 minutes, then transfer to a wire rack to cool completely.

✿ For the topping, whip the cream until it holds its shape. When the cupcakes are cool, use a piping bag fitted with a star nozzle to pipe the cream on top of each cupcake. To serve, top with a strawberry and dust with icing sugar. (Raspberries or other red berries can be substituted for strawberries.)

blueberry

18 APPROX

As a popular variation, make cranberry cupcakes by replacing the dried blueberries in this recipe with ready-to-eat dried cranberries.

you will need

200 g (7 oz) plain white flour

4 tsp baking powder

150 g (5½ oz) butter, softened

200 g (7 oz) caster sugar

2 large eggs

4 tbsp milk

150 g (5½ oz) ready-to-eat dried blueberries

sifted icing sugar, for dusting

❁ Preheat the oven to 180°C/350°F/Gas Mark 4. Line muffin pans with 18 fluted paper baking cups. Sift together the flour and baking powder.

❁ Put the butter and caster sugar in a large bowl and whisk until light and fluffy. Add the eggs, one at a time, beating well after each addition, then stir in the milk. Fold in the flour mixture, then gently fold in the blueberries.

❁ Fill each baking cup with the batter and bake in the oven for about 25 minutes until golden brown and firm to the touch. Leave in the pans for 10 minutes, then transfer to a wire rack to cool completely.

❁ Just before serving, dust the cupcakes with sifted icing sugar to decorate.

lemon ginger

Delicate and pretty, and with the addition of ginger, these attractive miniature cakes are a grown-up version of lemon butterfly cakes.

you will need

225 g (7 oz) plain white flour

2½ tsp baking powder

4 tsp ground ginger

225 g (8 oz) butter, softened

225 g (8 oz) caster sugar

4 eggs

4 tbsp milk

finely grated rind of 1 lemon

for the topping

175 g (6 oz) butter, softened

350 g (12 oz) icing sugar

2 tbsp lemon juice

5 pieces stem ginger
in syrup, cut into thin strips

sifted icing sugar, for dusting

✿ Preheat the oven to 190°C/375°F/Gas Mark 5. Line muffin pans with 18 fluted paper baking cups. Sift together the flour, baking powder and ginger.

✿ Put the butter and caster sugar in a large bowl and beat until light and fluffy. Add the eggs one at a time, beating well after each addition, then stir in the milk and lemon rind. Using a large metal spoon, fold in the flour mixture.

✿ Fill each baking cup with the batter and bake in the oven for about 25 minutes until golden brown and firm to the touch. Leave the cupcakes in the pans for 10 minutes, then transfer to a wire rack to cool completely.

✿ For the topping, beat the butter until light and fluffy. Sift in the icing sugar, then beat in the juice until smooth.

✿ Cut a circle from the top of each cupcake then cut the circles in half. Spread icing on the centre of each cupcake, then place strips of ginger on the centre of the icing to form butterfly bodies and a cake half on either side for wings. Dust with sifted icing sugar to serve.

mixed fruit

12 APPROX

Serve these miniature fruit-filled cakes as an alternative to Christmas cake. You can store the undecorated cakes in an airtight container up to a month before serving.

you will need

325 g (11½ oz) mixed dried fruits

6 tbsp sweet sherry

3 tbsp orange juice

140 g (5 oz) plain white flour

¼ tsp baking powder

1 tsp ground mixed spice

40 g (1½ oz) glacé cherries, finely chopped

115 g (4 oz) butter, softened

115 g (4 oz) soft dark brown sugar

2 large eggs

for the topping

450 g (1 lb) fondant icing

sifted icing sugar, for dusting

2½ tsp apricot jam

gold or silver dragées (cake decoration balls)

❀ Finely chop the mixed dried fruits in a food processor, then mix together in a bowl with the sherry and orange juice. Soak overnight.

❀ Preheat the oven to 150°C/300°F/Gas Mark 2. Line a muffin pan with 12 fluted foil baking cups and spray cups generously with a non-stick cooking spray. Sift together the dry ingredients. Add the cherries.

❀ Put the butter and brown sugar in a large bowl and whisk until light and fluffy, then gradually beat in the eggs. Fold in the flour mixture and soaked fruits.

❀ Fill each baking cup with the batter, level the surface, then make a slight hollow in the centre. Bake the cupcakes in the oven for about 1 hour. Cover the pan with a sheet of foil and leave to cool completely.

❀ To decorate, knead the fondant icing until pliable and roll out on a surface lightly dusted with icing sugar. Using a 7-cm (3-inch) round fluted cutter or other designs, cut out 12 shapes, re-rolling the icing as necessary.

❀ Heat the jam in a saucepan on the hob or in a microwave until melted. Brush over the cupcakes, press on an icing shape then decorate with dragées.

lemon cheesecake

10 APPROX

Soft, creamy cheesecake is always popular and, baked in individual cupcakes, is perfect served as a dessert or afternoon treat. Decorate with fresh fruit to make them extra special.

you will need

100 g (3½ oz) digestive biscuits, finely crushed

50 g (1¾ oz) butter

70 g (2½ oz) caster sugar

225 g (8 oz) full-fat soft cream cheese

2 eggs

105 ml (7 tbsp) soured cream

finely grated rind of 1 lemon

2 tsp lemon juice

3 tbsp plain white flour

10 sprigs fresh blackcurrants or redcurrants, or 10 small strawberries, to decorate

sifted icing sugar, for dusting

❀ Line a muffin pan with 10 fluted paper baking cups. Melt the butter, then add the crushed biscuits and 1 tablespoon of the caster sugar and mix well.

❀ Divide the mixture between the baking cups and press down firmly with the back of a teaspoon. Chill in the fridge while preparing the filling.

❀ Preheat the oven to 170°C/325°F/Gas Mark 3. Put the cream cheese, eggs and remaining caster sugar in a large bowl and whisk until smooth. Beat in the soured cream, lemon rind and juice, then beat in the flour until well combined.

❀ Fill each baking cup with the batter and bake in the oven for 30 minutes until set but not browned. Leave the cupcakes in the pan for 20 minutes, then transfer to a wire rack to cool completely.

❀ When cool, chill the cupcakes in the fridge for at least 3 hours before serving. To serve, decorate with fruit and dust with icing sugar.

apple sauce

These soft apple cupcakes with crumbly streusel topping are truly irresistible, especially when served warm – try with custard or ice cream as a comforting dessert.

you will need

175 g (6 oz) plain white flour

1¾ tsp baking powder

½ tsp cinnamon

½ tsp bicarbonate of soda

280-g (10-oz) jar Bramley apple sauce

55 g (2 oz) butter, softened

85 g (3 oz) demerara sugar

1 large egg

for the topping

50 g (1¾ oz) plain white flour

¼ tsp cinnamon

50 g (1¾ oz) demerara sugar

35 g (1¼ oz) butter, softened

❀ Preheat the oven to 180°C/350°F/Gas Mark 4. Line muffin pans with 14 fluted paper baking cups.

❀ For the topping, put the flour, cinnamon and sugar in a bowl. Cut the butter into small pieces and rub in, or blend in a food processor, with the flour mixture until the mixture resembles fine breadcrumbs. Set aside.

❀ For the cupcakes, sift together the flour, baking powder and cinnamon. Add the bicarbonate of soda to the apple sauce and stir until dissolved.

❀ Put the butter and sugar into a large bowl and then whisk until light and fluffy. Gradually beat in the egg. Using a large metal spoon, fold in the flour mixture and then the apple sauce.

❀ Fill each baking cup with the batter. Cover the surface of each with topping and press down gently. Bake the cupcakes in the oven for about 30 minutes or until risen and golden brown. Serve still slightly warm, or leave standing in the pans for 10 minutes, then transfer to a wire rack to cool completely.

pecan

Pecan nuts give these cupcakes a wonderfully moist texture, but ground walnuts can be used as an equally delicious alternative if preferred.

you will need

140 g (5 oz) plain white flour

1½ tsp baking powder

175 g (6 oz) pecan nuts

115 g (4 oz) butter, softened

200 g (7 oz) caster sugar

4 eggs

finely grated rind of 1 lemon

for the topping

175 g (6 oz) butter, softened

250 g (9 oz) icing sugar

2 tsp lemon juice

14 pecan nut halves

❀ Preheat the oven to 190°C/375°F/Gas Mark 5. Line muffin pans with 14 fluted paper baking cups. Sift together the flour and baking powder. Finely grind the pecans in a food processor using a pulsing action, taking great care not to overprocess them as this may cause the nuts to become oily.

❀ Put the butter and caster sugar in a large bowl and whisk until light and fluffy. Gradually beat in the eggs, one at a time, beating well after each addition, then beat in the lemon rind. Add the ground pecans, then fold in the flour mixture.

❀ Fill each baking cup with the batter and bake the cupcakes in the oven for about 25 minutes until golden brown and firm to the touch. Leave in the pans for 10 minutes, then transfer to a wire rack to cool completely.

❀ For the topping, beat the butter until light and fluffy. Sift in the icing sugar and add the lemon juice. Mix together until well combined.

❀ When the cupcakes are cool, pipe the icing on top of each cupcake using a piping bag fitted with a star nozzle and decorate each with a pecan half.

banana and walnut

Banana cupcakes are always the children's favourites, but these have the added luxury of walnuts for extra flavour and texture. Try snipped dates as an alternative to the walnuts.

you will need

225 g (8 oz) plain white flour

1¼ tsp baking powder

¼ tsp bicarbonate of soda

2 ripe bananas

115 g (4 oz) butter, softened

115 g (4 oz) caster sugar

½ tsp vanilla extract

2 eggs

4 tbsp soured cream

55 g (2 oz) walnut pieces, roughly chopped

for the topping

175 g (6 oz) butter, softened

350 g (12 oz) icing sugar

50 g (1¾ oz) walnut pieces, roughly chopped

❁ Preheat the oven to 190°C/375°F/Gas Mark 5. Line muffin pans with 14 fluted paper cups. Sift together the flour, baking powder and bicarbonate of soda. Mash the bananas with a fork in a separate bowl.

❁ Put the butter, caster sugar and vanilla extract in a large bowl and whisk until light and fluffy. Gradually beat in the eggs, then stir in the mashed bananas, soured cream and walnuts. Using a large metal spoon, fold in the flour mixture.

❁ Fill each baking cup with the batter and bake in the oven for about 25 minutes until risen, firm to the touch and golden brown. Leave the cupcakes in the pans for 10 minutes, then transfer to a wire rack to cool completely.

❁ For the topping, beat the butter until light and fluffy, then sift in the icing sugar and mix together well.

❁ When the cupcakes are cool, pipe the icing onto each cupcake, using a piping bag fitted with star nozzle and decorate with chopped walnuts.

peach

Take a bite of these deliciously moist cupcakes and you will have the sensation of eating a juicy peach! Slices of fresh fruit make a delicious accompaniment.

you will need

175 g (6 oz) plain white flour

2 tsp baking powder

10 canned peach slices in natural juice

175 g (6 oz) butter, softened

175 g (6 oz) caster sugar

2 large eggs

2 tbsp juice from the canned peaches

sifted icing sugar, for dusting

dragées

✿ Preheat the oven to 180°C/350°F/Gas Mark 4. Line muffin pans with 18 fluted paper baking cups. Sift together the flour and baking powder; finely chop the peach slices.

✿ Put the butter and caster sugar in a large bowl and whisk until light and fluffy. Gradually beat in the eggs one at a time, beating well after each addition. Using a large metal spoon, fold in the flour mixture, then the peaches and peach juice.

✿ Fill each baking cup with the batter and bake the cupcakes in the oven for about 25 minutes until golden brown and firm to the touch. Leave in the pans for 10 minutes, then transfer to a wire rack to cool completely.

✿ To serve, dust with sifted icing sugar and decorate with dragées.

almond and orange

These almond cupcakes, flavoured with fresh orange and topped with a delicious orange-flavoured icing, are for grown-ups – and they won't last long!

you will need

150 g (5½ oz) plain white flour

1¼ tsp baking powder

85 g (3 oz) butter, softened

100 g (3½ oz) caster sugar

1 large egg

finely grated rind of 1 orange

4 tbsp fresh orange juice

¼ tsp almond extract

55 g (2 oz) ground almonds

for the topping

115 g (4 oz) butter, softened

225 g (8 oz) icing sugar

finely grated rind of 1 orange

2 tsp fresh orange juice

few drops orange food colouring

25 g (1 oz) toasted flaked almonds

🌸 Preheat the oven to 180°C/350°F/Gas Mark 4. Line muffin pans with 10 fluted paper baking cups. Sift together the flour and baking powder.

🌸 Put the butter and caster sugar in a large bowl and whisk until light and fluffy. Gradually beat in the eggs, then the orange rind and juice, and almond extract. Stir in the ground almonds, then fold in the flour mixture.

🌸 Fill each baking cup with the batter and bake the cupcakes in the oven for about 25 minutes until golden brown and firm. Leave in the pans for 10 minutes, then transfer to a wire rack to cool completely.

🌸 For the topping, beat the butter until light and fluffy. Sift in the icing sugar, then add the rind and juice and beat until smooth and creamy. Add a few drops of food colouring to make the icing pale orange.

🌸 When the cupcakes are cool, pipe the icing on to each cupcake using a piping bag fitted with a star nozzle. To decorate, scatter over the flaked almonds.

chocolate brownies

12 APPROX

Serve these chocolate brownie cupcakes warm with real vanilla ice cream as a stylish dessert for a dinner party, or cold for any occasion. Chocolate lovers will be your friends for life!

you will need

115 g (4 oz) plain white flour

pinch of bicarbonate of soda

25 g (1 oz) tbsp cocoa powder

225 g (8 oz) plain chocolate

85 g (3 oz) butter

3 eggs

200 g (7 oz) caster sugar

100 g (3½ oz) walnut pieces, roughly chopped

🌸 Preheat the oven to 180°C/350°F/Gas Mark 4. Line a muffin pan with 12 fluted paper baking cups and spray cups generously with a non-stick cooking spray. Sift together the flour, bicarbonate of soda and cocoa powder.

🌸 Break the chocolate into a saucepan, add the butter and melt together over a gentle heat, stirring constantly, until smooth. Remove from heat.

🌸 Put the eggs and sugar in a large bowl and whisk. Add the flour mixture, then stir in the melted chocolate mixture and the walnuts.

🌸 Fill each baking cup with the batter and bake in the oven for about 30 minutes until a crust has formed but the cupcakes are still slightly moist in the centre. Serve the cupcakes warm, or leave in the pan for 10 minutes then transfer to a wire rack to cool completely.

chocolate courgette

12 APPROX

The addition of courgettes may sound unusual, but it partners wonderfully with chocolate and gives these cupcakes a wonderfully moist texture.

you will need

200 g (7 oz) plain white flour
1 tsp baking powder
½ tsp bicarbonate of soda
250 g (9 oz) firm courgettes
175 g (6 oz) plain chocolate
175 ml (6 fl oz) sunflower oil
2 large eggs
115 g (4 oz) caster sugar
sifted icing sugar, for dusting

❀ Preheat the oven to 180°C/350°F/Gas Mark 4. Line a muffin pan with 12 fluted paper baking cups. Sift together the flour, baking powder and bicarbonate of soda. Peel the courgettes, then grate them, squeezing out any excess moisture, and set aside on a plate.

❀ Break the chocolate into a small heatproof bowl set over a saucepan of gently simmering water; stir until melted and smooth. Remove from the heat and leave to cool slightly.

❀ Put the oil, eggs and caster sugar in a large bowl and whisk. Stir in the flour mixture, courgette and melted chocolate.

❀ Fill each baking cup with the batter and bake in the oven for about 25 minutes until firm to the touch. Leave the cupcakes in the pan for 10 minutes, then transfer to a wire rack to cool completely.

❀ When the cupcakes are cool, dust with icing sugar before serving.

cherry chocolate

12 APPROX

Cherries and chocolate are always a delicious combination, but, if you prefer, you can replace the cherry jam with strawberry or blackcurrant jam.

you will need

150 g (5½ oz) plain white flour
1½ tsp baking powder
100 g (3½ oz) plain chocolate
125 g (4½ oz) butter
250 g (9 oz) red cherry jam
125 g (4½ oz) caster sugar
2 large eggs

for the topping

100 g (3½ oz) plain chocolate
100 ml (3½ fl oz) double cream
12 maraschino or fresh cherries

❀ Preheat the oven to 180°C/350°F/Gas Mark 4. Line a muffin pan with 12 fluted paper baking cups. Sift together the flour and baking powder.

❀ Break the chocolate into a saucepan, add the butter and melt over a gentle heat, stirring constantly, until smooth. Pour into a bowl and leave to cool slightly.

❀ Add the jam, caster sugar and eggs, then beat with a wooden spoon until well mixed. Stir in the flour mixture.

❀ Fill each baking cup with the batter and bake in the oven for about 30 minutes until firm to the touch. Leave the cupcakes in the pan for 10 minutes, then transfer to a wire rack to cool completely.

❀ When the cupcakes are cool, make the topping. Melt the chocolate with the cream in a small saucepan over a gentle heat, stirring constantly, until smooth. Transfer to a bowl and, using an electric mixer, beat until thick and glossy.

❀ Spread the icing smoothly over the top of each cupcake and chill in the fridge for at least 1 hour before serving. Decorate with a cherry to serve.

mocha cappuccino

Topped with whipped cream and a fine dusting of cocoa, these appealing little cupcakes duplicate the enticing flavour of rich cappuccino coffee.

you will need

225 g (8 oz) plain white flour

2 tbsp cocoa powder

2 tbsp instant espresso coffee powder

85 g (3 oz) butter

85 g (3 oz) caster sugar

1 tbsp clear honey

200 ml (7 fl oz) water

1 tsp bicarbonate of soda

3 tbsp milk

1 large egg

for the topping

225 ml (8 fl oz) double cream

cocoa powder, for dusting

10 chocolate-covered coffee beans

✿ Preheat the oven to 180°C/350°F/Gas Mark 4. Line a muffin pan with 10 fluted paper baking cups. Sift together the flour and cocoa powder.

✿ Put the coffee, butter, caster sugar, honey and water together in a saucepan. Heat gently, stirring constantly, to dissolve the sugar. Bring to the boil, then reduce the heat and simmer for 5 minutes. Transfer to a large bowl and leave to cool. Dissolve the bicarbonate of soda in the milk.

✿ When butter mixture is cool, stir in the flour mixture, the bicarbonate of soda and milk, and the egg, then beat until smooth.

✿ Fill each baking cup with the batter and bake in the oven for about 25 minutes until firm to the touch. Leave the cupcakes in the pan for 10 minutes, then transfer to a wire rack to cool completely.

✿ For the topping, whip the cream until it holds its shape. Just before serving, spoon heaped teaspoonfuls on each cupcake, dust lightly with cocoa powder and add a chocolate-covered coffee bean.

white chocolate chip

12 APPROX

A silky white topping of white chocolate and cream cheese and a flourish of dark chocolate curls complement these classy cupcakes perfectly.

you will need

225 g (8 oz) plain white flour
2½ tsp baking powder
3½ tbsp cocoa powder
85 g (3 oz) butter, softened
100 g (3½ oz) caster sugar
2 eggs
4 tbsp) milk
55 g (2 oz) white chocolate chips

for the topping

225 g (8 oz) white chocolate
150 g (5½ oz) full-fat soft cream cheese
200 g (7 oz) plain chocolate

❁ Preheat the oven to 180°C/350°F/Gas Mark 4. Line a muffin pan with 12 fluted paper baking cups. Sift together the flour, baking powder and cocoa.

❁ Put the butter and caster sugar in a large bowl and whisk until light and fluffy, then gradually beat in the eggs. Fold in the flour mixture, milk and chocolate chips.

❁ Fill the baking cups with the batter and bake in the oven for about 25 minutes until firm to the touch. Leave the cupcakes in the pan for 10 minutes, then transfer to a wire rack to cool completely.

❁ For the topping, melt the white chocolate in a small heatproof bowl set over a saucepan of gently simmering water, stirring until smooth. Remove from the heat and leave to cool slightly. In a separate bowl, beat the cream cheese until smooth, then beat in the melted chocolate.

❁ Spread the icing on top of each cupcake. Chill them for at least 1 hour before serving. Decorate with shavings made using a potato peeler to shave curls from the plain chocolate bar.

cream-filled chocolate

10 APPROX

Filled with an indulgent swirl of whipped cream, these rich chocolate cakes are perfect treats for you and your guests. Decorate with a light dusting of icing sugar for the finishing touch.

you will need

150 g (5½ oz) plain white flour

1½ tsp baking powder

2 tbsp cocoa powder

25 g (1 oz) plain chocolate

115 g (4 oz) butter, softened

115 g (4 oz) caster sugar

2 eggs

for the filling

150 ml (¼ pint) double cream

sifted icing sugar, for dusting

✿ Preheat the oven to 180°C/350°F/Gas Mark 4. Line a muffin pan with 10 fluted paper baking cups. Sift together the flour, baking powder and cocoa powder.

✿ Break the chocolate into a heatproof bowl set over a saucepan of gently simmering water and melt, stirring constantly until smooth. Remove from the heat and leave to cool slightly.

✿ Put the butter and caster sugar in a large bowl and whisk until light and fluffy. Gradually beat in the eggs, one at a time, beating well after each addition, then beat in the melted chocolate. Fold in the flour mixture.

✿ Fill each baking cup with the batter and bake in the oven for about 25 minutes until firm to the touch. Leave the cupcakes in the pan for 10 minutes, then transfer to a wire rack to cool completely.

✿ Whip the cream until it holds its shape. Cut a circle from the top of each cake. Pipe a little cream into the centre using a piping bag fitted with a star nozzle, and top with a cake circle. Dust with icing sugar before serving.

chocolate fudge

Scrumptious chocolate cupcakes with a chocolate fudge topping can only be described as very tempting! For a birthday surprise, they're hard to beat.

you will need

115 g (4 oz) plain white flour
1 tbsp cocoa powder
100 ml (3½ fl oz) water
40 g (1½ oz) butter
3 tbsp caster sugar
½ tbsp golden syrup
1½ tbsp milk
½ tsp vanilla extract
½ tsp bicarbonate of soda

for the topping

50 g (1¾ oz) plain chocolate
2 tbsp water
25 g (1 oz) butter
175 g (6 oz) icing sugar

🌼 Preheat the oven to 180°C/350°F/Gas Mark 4. Line a muffin pan with 10 fluted paper baking cups. Sift together the flour and cocoa.

🌼 Heat together the water, butter, caster sugar and syrup in a saucepan, stirring constantly, until the sugar has dissolved. Bring to the boil, then reduce the heat and cook for 5 minutes. Remove from the heat and leave to cool.

🌼 Mix together the milk, vanilla and the bicarbonate of soda, stirring constantly to dissolve. Alternately pour the syrup mixture and milk into the flour mixture, beating well after each addition.

🌼 Fill each baking cup with the batter so they are no more than two-thirds full and bake them in the oven for about 25 minutes until firm to the touch. Leave the cupcakes in the pan for 10 minutes, then transfer to a wire rack to cool completely.

🌼 For the topping, melt the chocolate and butter together with the water in a heatproof bowl set over a saucepan of gently simmering water. Sift in the icing sugar and beat until smooth and thick. Spread the warm icing on top of each cupcake and leave to set before serving.

stencil suggestions

The designs illustrated here can be photocopied and the shapes cut out to make stencils. You can use paper for the stencils but card offers easier mobility. The best and safest way is to place your paper or card on a cutting mat and to carefully insert a craft knife at the edge of the design. Follow the shape of the design with your craft knife until you have completely removed the shape. Place your stencil over the cupcakes and give a generous dusting of sifted icing sugar or cocoa powder to add an attractive decoration and a finishing touch.

BELLS

FLOWERS

BUTTERFLY

BALLOONS

STARS

HOLLY

SHAMROCK

HEARTS

CHRISTMAS TREE

decorating ideas

Using a small round writing nozzle and a piping bag filled with icing or melted chocolate, you can create patterns on top of your cupcakes. Place the nozzle where you want the line to start and apply gentle pressure to the bag. As the icing flows out of the nozzle, lift the bag about 2 cm (1 inch) from the surface of the cupcake. Move your hand in the direction of the line. When the icing is about 1 cm (½ inch) from the end of the line, stop squeezing the bag and lower the tip of the nozzle to the surface of the cupcake. You can use the photos shown here as a guide to create patterns on your cupcakes for a final decoration.

HEART

FLOWER

SPIRAL